Faith Journey Testimony

Tasha Sellers

Table of Content

PREFACE

I come from a small town in Southern Illinois. Growing up, my mom made sure we had a church home to attend, and if we couldn't go, we watched sermons on TV on Sundays. At the age of 12, I accepted Jesus as my Lord and Savior. But like many people, I found myself falling short of God's glory on multiple occasions throughout my life. Despite these struggles, God's grace never left me.

At the age of 38, I experienced a powerful moment when God called me to serve as His prophet. I would like to clarify that my experience is with God, our Father in Heaven, the Father of Jesus, our Lord and Savior, who has called me to this divine assignment to serve as a vessel for His message. It's been a humbling journey, and I've come to understand that even in my shortcomings, God still chooses and uses us for His purpose.

The experiences I'm sharing with you are unique, however real! I must admit this comes with a lot of vulnerability. I've decided to document them in the hopes that by sharing my testimony, others will feel encouraged to speak freely about their own experiences with God. My prayer is that through my story, I can restore hope, help others grow in their faith, and maybe even lead someone to Christ.

By sharing my journey, I hope to show that no matter how far we've fallen, God's grace is always available, and His calling on our lives remains true. Through it all, I've learned that God has a purpose for each of us, no matter our past mistakes or struggles. My story is a testament to His faithfulness and the power of His presence in our lives.

Reflection Question:

What has been the most powerful lesson or insight that you've gained from your own relationship with God?

_____

_____

_____

_____

_____

_____

_____

_____

_____

_____

_____

_____

_____

_____

Key Scriptures:

"And we know that in all things God works for the good of those who love him, who have been called according to his purpose." – **Romans 8:28**

This scripture reflects the overarching theme of my story—God's ability to use every part of our journey for His greater plan. It sets the foundation for readers to understand that even our struggles have divine significance.

"God never said the journey would be easy, but He did say that the arrival would be worthwhile."
– Max Lucado.

CHAPTER 1

Divine Intervention

Introduction

This chapter explores how God's intervention can transform our lives, even in the darkest moments of despair. I share the turning point when God revealed His presence to me during a challenging time in my marriage, setting me on the path toward my divine calling.

After nine years of marriage, I found myself facing something I never thought I would: the possibility of divorce. My husband and I had been in constant disagreement, and it seemed like our marriage was coming to an end. We made the difficult decision to separate.

During this time apart, I struggled deeply with the idea of living according to God's Word. I knew that if I divorced my husband, I would be considered a divorcee in the eyes of God and would have to remain that way, unless my husband passed away. I truly wanted my marriage to work, and I longed for companionship, for it saddened me. Emotionally, I was on a rollercoaster—some days good, other days bad.

Throughout this time, my mother, my sister Tara, and my brother Jules called almost every day for over a month to check in on me. Their support helped keep me going. I also made a conscious decision to strengthen my prayer life. Each day, I prayed for guidance, strength, and wisdom. I began to ask God to take control of my life, to use me as He saw fit, and to push me out of my comfort zone. Little did I know, He was about to do just that!

For weeks, I had been struggling to sleep. Every night, I would wake up between 3:00 a.m. and 4:00 a.m. and couldn't understand why. One day, as I was scrolling through social media, I came across a message from a pastor titled *"Signs You Have Been Chosen."* Something about the title caught my attention, so I listened to the message. The pastor said that if you're waking up early in the morning like I had been, it's a sign that God is trying to communicate with you. He encouraged people to stay awake and wait on God's revelation.

So, I decided to do just that.

In the early morning hours of November 22, 2023, the Lord appeared. It was an experience like no other. As I lay on the floor, it felt as though He was a physician, examining my entire body from head to toe. I knew this was a supernatural encounter—my physical strength could not stop it from happening. This moment lasted for over three hours, and it was on this day that God revealed my calling to me.

The Lord told me that He had chosen me to be a prophet. Overwhelmed and confused, I kept asking Him, "Why me?" His response was always the same: "Why not you?" One day, He elaborated, explaining that I have always been called for His purpose. He was simply waiting for the right time to reveal it to me.

The Lord reminded me of my pure heart as a child, which has carried over into my adulthood journey. I have always desired the best for others. Despite the sins I had committed throughout my life, He assured me that He was judging my heart—a reflection of my genuine desires and purpose.

What makes this experience even more incredible is that just four days earlier, on November 18, 2023, the Lord had already made His presence powerfully known. For the first time in my life, while listening to worship music and praising God, I began to speak in tongues, a language I did not understand. I tried to stop, but I had no control over it. The experience lasted for over an hour. During this time, my 7-year-old son was in the living room watching TV, and I was so worried he might come in and be confused by what was happening. But he never entered the room. Every time I tried to stand or compose myself, I found myself falling back to the ground, as the Lord's presence remained with me.

The pinched nerve I had struggled with for seven years had healed entirely after the experience finally ended, I realized. The experience was especially significant to me because seven represents completion in Scripture. But it was on November 22 that the Lord made it clear: He was calling me to something greater!

This experience led to several more encounters that I will share, but it's also important to note that this was the first step in the Lord's work to restore my marriage—what I would later come to call "Divine Intervention."

Reflection Question:

Have you ever experienced a time when God was trying to get your attention? How did you respond?

_____

_____

_____

_____

_____

_____

_____

_____

_____

_____

_____

_____

_____

_____

Key Scriptures:

"For I know the plans I have for you," declares the Lord, "plans to prosper you and not to harm you, plans to give you hope and a future."
-Jeremiah 29:11

This verse emphasizes that God's intervention is intentional and rooted in His perfect plan, even during times of despair.

"The Lord is close to the brokenhearted and saves those who are crushed in spirit." - **Psalm 34:18***:*

This scripture reflects God's presence during my marital struggles and separation, offering comfort and hope.

"The Lord came and stood there, calling as the other times, 'Samuel! Samuel!' Then Samuel said, 'Speak, for your servant is listening."
- 1 Samuel 3:10

This verse parallels my decision to stay awake and listen to God when I began waking up early, symbolizing my obedience to His call.

"When God gives you a new beginning, it starts with an ending. Be thankful for closed doors. They often guide us to the right one." – **Unknown.**

CHAPTER 2

He Restored My Marriage

Introduction

In this chapter, I recount how God healed and restored my broken marriage, showing that even in the darkest times, His power and grace can bring about transformation and renewal.

Before delving into the specific miracles I've experienced, I believe it's important to share the story of how God miraculously restored my marriage. Without a doubt, this has been one of the most profound blessings in my life.

At a time when I was certain my marriage was beyond repair and divorce seemed inevitable, I prayed earnestly and asked God to comfort me, strengthen me, and guide me. Even in the midst of my storms, I still had obligations and daily responsibilities. Being a mother of three children, I knew I had to fight through the hurt that came along with dealing with a breakup, as I needed to be mentally and emotionally available for them. When relationships fail, there are several casualties. The kids had been deeply impacted by our decision to split, and struggled with the reality of our broken home. Convinced that my marriage was over, I took the step of consulting with a divorce lawyer. In my mind, it was the only option left. The pain, misunderstandings, and emotional distance had taken their toll. It felt like we had exhausted every possibility for reconciliation, and the only path forward was to end what had once been a sacred union.

But God had a different plan, one neither of us could have imagined. While both of us had come to the decision that our marriage was over, God was quietly working behind the scenes, orchestrating something far greater than we could see.

Thanksgiving was less than a week away, and this would be the first time we would be spending the holiday apart. Although my husband and I were separated, he agreed to ride with me to pick our son up from college for Fall break. It was during this drive that the Lord showed His presence once more, taking control of my movements while I was behind the wheel. My husband, concerned, offered to take over driving, but the Lord had me decline and continue. That's when it hit me: God had the power to take control of my physical body even when I wasn't in a spiritual state, as we might define it in moments of the Holy Spirit's manifest presence. God's presence became so undeniable that it left my husband in awe, and what he witnessed opened the door for some challenging yet necessary conversations.

Over the course of several days, profound revelations and painful truths emerged. God's light began to shine into areas of our hearts where there had been confusion, anger, and fear. It became clear that the enemy had worked tirelessly to deceive us and create the illusion that there was no hope left for our marriage.

With God at the center, we began to experience breakthroughs, new levels of understanding, healing, and transparency. We prayed together, sometimes with tears streaming down our faces, as we surrendered our marriage to God's will. What had once felt impossible was now becoming a reality: the restoration of our marriage. God's work didn't happen overnight, but it began with that moment of divine intervention and continues to this day.

When we invite God into our struggles, He can transform even the most broken situations. Have faith that His timing is perfect.

Stay with me as I share more about the specific miracles and breakthroughs that followed, and how God continued to work in our lives.

Reflection Question:

When have you faced a situation that seemed beyond repair, and how did you experience God's presence or guidance working behind the scenes to bring healing or restoration?

_____

_____

_____

_____

_____

_____

_____

_____

_____

_____

_____

_____

_____

Key Scriptures:

*"I will repay you for the years the
locusts have eaten."* - **Joel 2:25**:

This verse reflects God's promise to restore what seemed lost in my marriage, showing His ability to redeem even the most broken situations.

*"So they are no longer two, but one flesh.
Therefore, what God has joined together,
let no one separate."* - **Matthew 19:6**

This scripture highlights the sacredness of my marriage and God's desire for its restoration.

*"Be joyful in hope, patient in affliction,
faithful in prayer."* - **Romans 12:12**

This verse aligns with my journey of prayer and faithfulness during the difficult times in my marriage.

*"A successful marriage requires falling in
love many times, always with the same
person."* – **Mignon McLaughlin.**

CHAPTER 3

Miracles Are Happening

Introduction

This chapter highlights the tangible, miraculous ways in which God continues to show His power in my life, reinforcing the truth that nothing is beyond His ability to restore and transform.

Once called for an assignment, God made it clear exactly who was speaking through me. While the confirmation was not needed for my faith, the Lord reassured me in several ways. I began to experience, witness, and see multiple miracles daily.

For years, I suffered from what most would call carpal tunnel syndrome in my right hand due to countless hours of typing during my work in customer service. My fingers on that hand were bent into the typing position, seemingly locked there. But on November 25th, 2023, the Lord strengthened my hand. My fingers straightened. Also on this day, I inherited the ability to write with my left hand, a skill I had never possessed before. It was a small but profound physical transformation that reaffirmed my faith.

Another significant moment occurred when my husband and I visited Zales to upgrade our wedding rings. God guided every step of the process, culminating in a miraculous financial provision that defied human logic.

Before we went to the store, the Lord instructed me to put the purchase under my name. When we arrived, He provided further guidance: He instructed both my husband and me to choose the rings we wanted without worrying about the price. After selecting the perfect rings, I followed the Lord's instructions and asked the store clerk to check my eligibility for a Zales credit card. When the clerk ran my credit, I got approved for a substantial amount, but it wasn't enough to cover the full purchase.

Feeling uncertain, I asked the clerk to run my husband's credit, even though the Lord had directed me otherwise. He got approved for an amount large enough to combine our purchases on credit. However, as the clerk processed the transaction, something miraculous occurred. She began with my account, entering the total cost of the rings, and was surprised to find that the system allowed the full amount to go through under my name, even though my approved limit didn't cover it. Concerned, she called Zales' credit line for support.

While she was on the phone, the Lord spoke to me and said, "I just performed a miracle. I told you the purchase was to go under your name only." When the clerk finished the call, she told us she had never seen anything like this before. The credit line representative confirmed that the transaction was approved and that I was "good to go," despite the discrepancy in the credit limit. This moment served as a powerful reminder to trust God's guidance, regardless of how things may seem.

While the last miracle I shared may seem materialistic, it serves as a powerful testimony to God's limitless power.

For my birthday, the Lord blessed me with several wonders in the sky, ensuring that my family was there to witness them with me. One of the first miracles was a cloud that transformed into the shape of a fish. God's message to me was clear: "You will never go hungry again." The powerful reminder of Jesus' miracle of feeding the multitude with two loaves of bread and a fish.

Next, he turned the sky red, symbolizing the blood of Jesus, the ultimate sacrifice for our sins. My family and I were astonished by God's display, and it continued. He revealed three stars in the otherwise clear night sky, explaining that they represented Him, His Son Jesus, and the Holy Spirit. For at least an hour, God continued to show us His works, leaving us in awe. The performance concluded with perhaps the most astonishing act: the moon itself disappeared from the sky. We watched as the Lord summoned the moon, and it vanished before our eyes, a sight I will never forget!

While some may find these accounts hard to believe, I feel deeply grateful that the Lord chose my family and me to witness such miraculous events. These moments have not only strengthened my faith but have also reinforced the importance of trusting in God's plan, regardless of how things may seem. In my next sharing, I'll recount the blessings that he bestowed on my family.

Reflection Question:

What miracles, big or small, have you witnessed in your own life?
How did they impact your faith?

_____

_____

_____

_____

_____

_____

_____

_____

_____

_____

_____

_____

_____

_____

_____

Key Scriptures:

"Jesus replied, 'What is impossible with man is possible with God." - **Luke 18:27**:

This scripture underscores the miraculous healing of my pinched nerve, my newfound ability to write with my left hand, and the provision for upgrading our wedding rings.

"So do not fear, for I am with you; do not be dismayed, for I am your God. I will strengthen you and help you; I will uphold you with my righteous right hand." - **Isaiah 41:10**

This verse reflects the miraculous ways God has shown His power in my life, especially in moments of healing and guidance.

The heavens declare the glory of God; the skies proclaim the work of his hands." - **Psalm 19:1**:

This scripture connects beautifully to the miraculous signs in the sky, such as the fish-shaped cloud and the disappearing moon, as testimonies of God's glory.

"Faith sees the invisible, believes the unbelievable, and receives the impossible." – **Corrie Ten Boom.**

CHAPTER 4

Blessings by Default

Introduction

Life is often a journey of unexpected turns, where blessings and challenges intertwine. As I grew deeper in my relationship with God, He revealed that my journey was not just about personal growth but also about being a vessel of His blessings for others. However, before these blessings could unfold, I had to trust His process, even when it meant letting go of people and situations I held dear. This chapter shares the miraculous ways God's favor touched not only my life but also the lives of those connected to me.

As God filled me with His presence, He made it abundantly clear that His blessings would not be limited to me alone; anyone closely connected to me would also experience His favor. However, He also warned me that this journey would include challenging moments, as he needed to separate me from individuals who were not meant to accompany me. He led me to the Book of Job and explained that, like Job, I would face trials. But unlike Job, Satan could not harm me—he could attempt to intimidate me, but he would not have the power to touch me.

This process of separation was difficult, as no one was exempt from being removed from my husband's and my life, including long-time friends/associates and family members. The Lord revealed that He was not judging anyone for their sins but was instead looking at their hearts and true intentions. While these severed relationships were painful, they ultimately made sense as part of His divine plan. Through it all, the Lord stayed true to His word: those around me began to witness God's blessings unfolding.

Miracles Within My Household

Before sharing the blessings others have experienced outside my household, I would like first to highlight a remarkable event that occurred in my own home. One of the most extraordinary miracles involved my 7-year-old son, who had been diagnosed with autism and faced challenges with verbal communication and self-expression. For two years, He attended private speech therapy sessions twice a week, along with sessions provided at his school, while I fervently prayed for his breakthrough.

One morning at 3:13 a.m., the Lord's presence manifested powerfully. He told me he would work through me to heal my son. As my son slept, God worked through me pressing down on his mouth and tongue. He assured me that the change would be noticeable and that his speech therapist, whom he met with twice a week, would see the difference but would not be able to explain it.

Immediately afterwards, my husband and I noticed a significant improvement in my son's speech. Although he still had some challenges with enunciation, his clarity had significantly improved, and we could understand most of what he said. Less than a month later, his therapist informed me that he had graduated from the private speech program, having met all the required benchmarks. This miraculous transformation is just one of the many blessings that have unfolded in our home.

Another profoundly meaningful experience occurred when the Lord called my husband's late mother to speak through me to him. Through this divine encounter, my husband found the closure he had been seeking. There were two separate occasions. Afterward, the Lord explained that He would no longer summon her, as she needed to transition over fully.

Other miracles included the Lord teaching me to praise dance, rebuking demonic spirits from our household, revealing my husband's calling to become a deacon, and guiding my husband and me through home renovations and the creation of a gated garden. There are other miraculous moments that I have not included in this text, which have also occurred and impacted our lives forever.

Blessings Beyond My Household

As promised, God's blessings have also extended to my family. Here's an account of how the Lord blessed my sister and her family. To her amazement, God revealed that her 2-year-old son was experiencing delays in speech and cognitive development. Although my sister, a busy mother of four, had not noticed any warning signs, she trusted God's guidance and sought professional advice, which confirmed that her son was behind the percentile. As a result, her son enrolled in a specialized program, which covered most of the expenses, following this confirmation. Remarkably, she discovered that he had just barely made the enrollment deadline.

Another significant blessing revealed through God's guidance was His instruction for my sister to find a church home. While she had a relationship with Him, He pointed out that her children did not know Him and urged her to visit local churches until He confirmed the right one. During this time, the Lord shared that her oldest daughter would ask to get baptized. True to His word, He confirmed which church she should join. Shortly after they joined the church, her oldest daughter expressed the desire to get baptized. Every detail unfolded precisely as the Lord had revealed.

One final blessing I'll share about her household is her journey to getting a new car. She often mentioned needing one but was worried about affording the monthly payments. God reassured her that she could comfortably manage a $200 monthly payment and promised she would have a new vehicle by summer. When her current car became increasingly unreliable, she started searching for a new vehicle and found a 2011 Nissan Pathfinder that caught her eye. Before moving forward, she called to seek guidance from the Lord on whether or not she was making the right decision. God guided her away from that vehicle and directed her to a 2017 Nissan Pathfinder, not far from her home, which was priced lower than the older model vehicle she was looking to purchase. Trusting His direction, my sister made the trip, and the purchase went smoothly.

Similarly, my mom had long faced challenges with unreliable transportation. One evening, God prompted me to search online for a Chrysler Pacifica and to ask my mom if she liked it. When she said yes, things began to fall into place. God directed me to a specific 2018 Chrysler Pacifica, which had just dropped in price by $4,000 a few days earlier. Following His guidance, my mom traveled to Tennessee and, with my assistance, purchased the van. This dependable vehicle became a tremendous blessing, especially as she had recently taken on temporary guardianship of her great-grandchildren.

Reflection Question:

As you reflect on the blessings in your own life, who has God placed around you to receive His favor through your obedience?

_____

_____

_____

_____

_____

_____

_____

_____

_____

_____

_____

_____

_____

_____

_____

Key Scriptures:

"Have you not put a hedge around him and his household and everything he has? You have blessed the work of his hands, so that his flocks and herds are spread throughout the land."
- Job 1:10:

This verse parallels God's blessings on my family.

"Take delight in the Lord, and he will give you the desires of your heart." **- Psalm 37:4**

This scripture aligns with the blessings my family experienced, from my mother's new van to my sister's church home and my son's speech breakthrough.

"I will make you into a great nation, and I will bless you; I will make your name great, and you will be a blessing." **- Genesis 12:2**

This verse reflects the blessings God has extended through my obedience, which has impacted those closely connected to me.

*"Whoever welcomes a prophet as a prophet
will receive a prophet's reward, and
whoever welcomes a righteous person as
a righteous person will receive a righteous
person's reward."* **- Matthew 10:41**

This verse reveals that even through the hardships of separation, as God removed those not meant to walk this path with me, it reflected His divine purpose. While it was difficult, these moments of refinement made sure that those who remained could fully receive His blessings and the rewards of their faithfulness.

*"Blessings flow when we walk in obedience,
trusting that God's plan is greater than
anything we could imagine."* **– Unknown.**

CHAPTER 5

The Lord Disciplines
the ones He loves

Introduction

Discipline is often a misunderstood aspect of love. Many of us embrace the idea of God's blessings with gratitude, but we usually wrestle with the notion of His correction. We might see discipline as punishment, forgetting that it is an act of love and care, a way for God to mold us into the people He created us to be.

In this chapter, we will explore the concept of divine discipline, its purpose, and how it reflects the depth of God's love for us. Just as a parent disciplines their child for their growth and well-being, our heavenly Father corrects us out of a desire to draw us closer to Him and to help us reflect His character. While the process can be challenging, it is a gift that brings wisdom, humility, and spiritual maturity.

Let us open our hearts to understand how God's discipline works in our lives, how it aligns with His command to love, and how it ultimately strengthens our faith and relationships.

As followers of Christ, we often welcome God's blessings with open hearts. Yet, we sometimes struggle to accept that the same God who blesses us also corrects us. Discipline is a profound expression of love, although it can be difficult to reconcile.

> *"My son, do not despise the Lord's discipline,*
> *and do not resent His rebuke, because the*
> *Lord disciplines those He loves, as a father the*
> *son He delights in." -* **Proverbs 3:11-12**

Consider the role of a parent. We teach our children the difference between right and wrong, and when they stray from those values, we discipline them—not out of anger, but out of love and a desire to guide them. It's not an easy task; discipline can be painful for both the giver and the receiver. Yet, as parents, we remind ourselves that these moments are necessary for growth. Similarly, our heavenly Father disciplines us to refine and strengthen us, not to harm us.

One way God lovingly corrects us is by inviting us to turn inward, reflecting on our own shortcomings rather than focusing on the flaws of others. Self-reflection is one of the most challenging but transformative aspects of faith. Even for those deeply rooted in God's Word, examining our own hearts can be an uncomfortable experience. Yet, it is through this process that we grow closer to God's character.

> *"Why do you look at the speck of sawdust in your brother's eye and pay no attention to the plank in your own eye? How can you say to your brother, 'Let me take the speck out of your eye,' when all the time there is a plank in your own eye? You hypocrite, first take the plank out of your own eye, and then you will see clearly to remove the speck from your brother's eye."* - **Matthew 7:3-5**

God's discipline may come in many forms—circumstances that stretch us, relationships that challenge us, or gentle convictions that nudge us toward repentance. At the core of this discipline is love. God does not call out our sins to condemn us but to guide us toward a better path. As He has worked in my life, I've come to see His correction as an act of grace.

One of the most profound lessons I've learned is that every action and every word should be rooted in love. This principle aligns with the greatest commandments in the Bible:

> *"Love the Lord your God with all your heart and with all your soul and with all your mind." This is the first and greatest commandment. And the second is like it: "Love your neighbor as yourself."*
> **- Matthew 22:37-39**

In reflecting on these truths, I've recognized how often human nature—our "flesh"—leads us astray. We are quick to act on impulse, speak in frustration, or make decisions driven by selfish desires, often without considering the impact of our actions on others.

> *"For the flesh desires what is contrary to the Spirit, and the Spirit what is contrary to the flesh. They are in conflict with each other, so you are not to do whatever you want."* **- Galatians 5:17**

God's presence in my life has taught me the importance of pausing, seeking understanding, and responding thoughtfully. For example, in moments of disagreement, I've learned not to speak the first thing that comes to mind. Instead, I strive to fully receive and reflect on what others are saying before I respond. This practice, while not always easy, is one way I've embraced the discipline of love.

Through His correction, God challenges each of us to consider: Are our words and actions motivated by love? This question has become a guiding principle in my life, shaping how I navigate my relationships and how I grow in faith.

> *"No discipline seems pleasant at the time, but painful. Later on, however, it produces a harvest of righteousness and peace for those who have been trained by it."* - **Hebrews 12:11**

Let us remember that God's discipline is never a sign of His absence but rather evidence of His deep and abiding love. Just as a loving parent seeks the best for their child, so too does our Lord seek to shape us into reflections of His goodness and grace.

Reflection Question:

How have you experienced God's discipline in your life? How has it shaped your relationship with Him and your understanding of His love?

_____

_____

_____

_____

_____

_____

_____

_____

_____

_____

_____

_____

_____

_____

CHAPTER 6

God's Sense of Humor

Introduction

This chapter explores a facet of God that is often overlooked—His sense of humor. While we often think of God as loving, merciful, and just, we sometimes forget that He also has a playful and joyful nature. As I deepened my relationship with Him, I began to see glimpses of this humor in our interactions. It's a testament to the personal and intimate connection He desires to have with each of us. These moments of divine laughter not only brought me closer to Him but also reminded me of how truly relatable He is.

One of the most gratifying aspects of being on assignment for the Lord is experiencing His incredible sense of humor. We often hear that we are made in God's image, and the more I grow in my relationship with Him, the more I realize how true that is. As I've drawn closer to Him, He has revealed more of His character to me, including His playful and clever nature.

The Lord has brought so much joy to my life through His witty remarks and lighthearted interactions. These moments of humor have been a balm for my soul, reminding me of His closeness and the depth of His personality. The more I interact with Him, the more I understand how we truly reflect His image in ways we may not always recognize. I often find myself marveling at how fortunate I am to witness this side of Him.

God's humor often catches me off guard, which makes it all the more delightful. It's as though He knows the exact moment to make me laugh, filling my heart with joy and reassurance. The Bible tells us that if we open the door and invite Him in, He will eat with us. But that's just the beginning. His presence in our daily lives is so much more dynamic and personal than we can imagine.

There are times when I find myself having out-loud conversations with the Lord. What started as occasional chats has now become a regular part of my life. Sometimes, when I don't feel His immediate presence, I'll call out to Him like a child seeking attention from a parent: "Hey, are you still there?" Without fail, He responds in His own way, letting me know He's always with me.

For anyone wondering if God has a sense of humor, He absolutely does! His humor is a beautiful reminder of His intimacy with us, His love for us, and His desire to share in every aspect of our lives, even the moments of laughter.

Reflection Question:

Have you experienced moments when God's humor brought joy or reassurance into your life? How do these interactions shape your understanding of His closeness and personality?

_____

_____

_____

_____

_____

_____

_____

_____

_____

_____

_____

_____

_____

_____

Key Scriptures:

"A cheerful heart is good medicine, but a crushed spirit dries up the bones." - **Proverbs 17:22**

This verse reminds us that laughter and joy, even when Inspired by God, it is a gift that uplifts and heals us.

"A time to weep and a time to laugh, a time to mourn and a time to dance." - **Ecclesiastes 3:4**

This scripture reflects the balance God brings to our lives, including moments of humor and joy.

"Our mouths were filled with laughter, our tongues with songs of joy. Then it was said among the nations, 'The Lord has done great things for them." - **Psalm 126:2**

This verse highlights how God's presence can fill us with laughter and joy, serving as a testament to His goodness.

"So I say to you: Ask and it will be given to you; seek and you will find; knock and the door will be opened to you. For everyone who asks receives; the one who seeks finds; and to the one who knocks, the door will be opened." - **Luke 11:9-10**

This passage ties in beautifully with the idea of opening our hearts to God, allowing Him to show us His love, humor, and presence.

By reflecting on God's humor and embracing the joy He brings, we can deepen our relationship with Him. Laughter, like love, is a way He connects with us, reminding us that He is not only our Savior but also our companion in every season of life.

CHAPTER 7

My Assignment

Introduction

Throughout my journey of faith, I've learned that God calls us to assignments not just for the benefit of others but also to shape and refine us. Each mission He gives is an opportunity to grow in obedience, humility, and love. Accepting these assignments often means stepping out of our comfort zones, trusting in His wisdom, and embracing the unknown.

This chapter is a testimony of one of those assignments—a powerful example of how God uses ordinary people to fulfill His extraordinary plans. I hope that this story not only inspires but also encourages you to be attentive to God's calling in your own life.

As mentioned in Chapter 1, when the Lord graced me with His presence, He revealed my calling. During this divine conversation, He explained to me that I had been given the gift of prophecy, a messenger for whomever He instructed me to speak to. From that moment on, I was, in the eyes of the Lord, a prophet. While some may use the feminine term "prophetess" because I am a woman, God reminded me that the roles are the same.

When I first received this anointing, I was extremely nervous. Like many, I hesitated and questioned, "You want me to go to *whom* and say *what*?" I asked, "Lord, what if they don't believe me?" The Lord, in His wisdom, assured me: "Just speak the words I give you. They may not make sense to you, but the intended recipient will know that the message is from Me."

> *"Do not be afraid of them, for I am with you and will rescue you," declares the Lord.* - **Jeremiah 1:8**

When delivering a message from God, I always ensure that it begins with, "The Lord says to tell you this." It is essential to clarify that I am merely the messenger, never claiming credit for God's work. I've learned that God often reveals only what is necessary, avoiding overly sensitive information about the person when I am sent to speak with them. The messages may seem simple, but they carry profound substance.

There have been times when I delivered a message, and the recipient immediately elaborated on its meaning.

We must also understand that sometimes God may use you to deliver a message without engaging in a verbal conversation. I was invited to a church's Friends and Family Day by an acquaintance I had met through a relative. Initially, I thought, "Thanks, but no thanks," assuming she hoped I would join her church even though I already had a church home. But the Lord had other plans. He told me clearly, "You will attend this service." Obediently, I went with my husband that Sunday.

> *"Trust in the Lord with all your heart and lean not on your own understanding; in all your ways submit to him, and he will make your paths straight."* - **Proverbs 3 5-6**

Upon our arrival, everyone was welcoming and kind. The host had donuts for guests before the service started, and the woman who invited me introduced us to several members. During this time, an older woman, who appeared to be struggling with a mental disability, quietly approached and exchanged a few words with us.

As the service began, the pastor invited those who wished to come forward to give thanks at the altar while the choir sang. At that moment, the Lord spoke: "Tasha, go to the front of the church now." Initially, I hesitated, questioning if I had heard Him correctly. But he repeated, "Go to the front and stand beside the older woman." Nervous yet obedient, I walked to the front and stood next to her.

"My sheep listen to my voice; I know them,
and they follow me." - **John 10:27**

The Lord instructed, "Reach out and take her hand. She won't resist." I did as I was told, holding her hand and waiting for further guidance. After a few minutes, the Lord said I could return to my seat.

Later, He explained the purpose of this assignment. Although a good pastor led the church, there was an opportunity for growth in how the congregation demonstrated love and care, particularly to those facing challenges, such as the older woman. She had been overlooked, her presence brushed aside due to her mental struggles. My task was to visibly show an act of love and connection, prompting the congregation to reflect on how they treated her.

"A new command I give you: Love one
another. As I have loved you, so you must
love one another." - **John 13:34**

After the service, a man sitting near me commented on how he could see I was highly anointed. The woman who invited me asked if I would return for another service, but the Lord made it clear that my assignment at that church was complete.

This experience, like many others, has deepened my understanding of one of God's greatest commandments: to love.

Reflecting on this assignment, I'm reminded that God's plans often go beyond what we can see. Initially, I thought I was attending the service as a guest, but God used me to fulfill a purpose far greater than I had expected. This experience taught me that obedience to His voice is crucial, even when His instructions seem unclear or straightforward.

Sometimes, God's assignments are not about grand gestures but about small acts of love and kindness that create ripple effects in the hearts of others. Through this moment, God revealed the importance of seeing and valuing everyone, especially those society may overlook.

> *"Whatever you did for one of the least*
> *of these brothers and sisters of mine,*
> *you did for me."* - **Matthew 25:40**

I also learned that God's work through us is not about recognition or personal gain but about glorifying Him. As we serve others in love, we become His hands and feet, reflecting His character to the world.

If there is one takeaway from this experience, it's that God's assignments, no matter how small they seem, are opportunities for us to grow in faith, humility, and love.

CONCLUSION

As I conclude my testimony about my faith, my journey, and experiences with God, I want to encourage anyone who has not accepted Jesus as their Lord and Savior to take that step of faith. The greatest gift we can receive is eternal life.

> *"For God so loved the world that he gave his one and only Son, that whoever believes in him shall not perish but have eternal life."* - **John 3:16**

> *"For what does it profit a man to gain the whole world and forfeit his soul?"* - **Luke 9:25**

In a world filled with distractions, social media, advanced technology, and political motivations, it is easy to lose focus on what truly matters: saving your soul. If you struggle to understand God's word, draw closer to Him, and He will reveal its meaning to you.

Accepting Jesus as your Savior opens the door to eternal life, but our actions must align with God's will. Many people sin and ask for forgiveness without a true desire to change, expecting the Lord to overlook their actions. It is essential to examine ourselves, ensuring we do not become like the Pharisees, those who understand God's word but are unwilling to make the necessary changes due to selfish desires.

*"Therefore, if anyone is in Christ, the new creation
has come: The old has gone, the new is here!"*
- 2 Corinthians 5:17

One day, all of humanity will stand before God and account for their sins. My prayer is that you find yourself on the right side of His judgment.

My testimony brings hope to those who feel hopeless, joy to those in sorrow, humility to those struggling with pride, and, above all, a message filled with love.

Faith Journey Testimony Reflection Questions

1. Have you ever felt God prompting you to do something that seemed uncomfortable or unclear? How did you respond?

_____

_____

_____

_____

_____

_____

_____

_____

_____

_____

_____

_____

_____

_____

_____

_____

2. What does it mean to you to show love and kindness to those who are often overlooked by society?

_____

_____

_____

_____

_____

_____

_____

_____

_____

_____

_____

_____

_____

_____

_____

_____

_____

3.	How can you better tune your heart and mind to hear and obey God's voice in your daily life?

_____

_____

_____

_____

_____

_____

_____

_____

_____

_____

_____

_____

_____

_____

_____

4. Reflect on a time when God used you to bless someone else. How did that experience impact your faith journey?

_____

_____

_____

_____

_____

_____

_____

_____

_____

_____

_____

_____

_____

_____

_____

_____

5. What steps can you take to ensure you remain humble and obedient as you carry out God's will in your life?

_____

_____

_____

_____

_____

_____

_____

_____

_____

_____

_____

_____

_____

_____

_____

_____

POWERFUL PRAYERS: PREPARE FOR A BREAKTHROUGH!

Dealing with Rejection

Lord, I ask for Your help in releasing the fear of rejection that I carry. Heal the wounds from past trauma and hurt, whether from childhood or relationships, that have affected my confidence and self-esteem. I pray, Lord, that You not only help me understand my true worth but also guide me to love myself fully, embracing both my strengths and imperfections. Help me overcome the insecurities that overshadow the person I am. Heal the scars of psychological abuse, and restore my sense of peace and confidence. In Jesus' name, I pray. Amen!

Self-Reflection

Lord, please reveal to me any actions I may have taken that have opened the door to the challenges I'm facing. Grant me wisdom and understanding as I navigate these trials and tribulations. I take full responsibility for my part in the struggles I face, and I seek Your help to overcome them. I know that Satan is the true enemy behind my difficulties, and I ask in Jesus' name for Your deliverance from his attempts to make me suffer. Lord, surround me with Your protection and build a wall around my family, my mind, and my heart, blocking the devil's schemes. Your word says, "Ask, and it will be given; seek, and you will find; knock, and the door will be opened." I humbly bow before You in worship, praising Your name and declaring victory over my burdens. In Jesus' name, I pray. Amen!

Transform My Life

Lord, help me to stop living my life in shallow waters. I invite you into my life to take complete control. Do whatever is needed in my career, relationships, and business ventures, according to Your divine plan. Teach me not to rely on my own understanding or emotions, but to listen closely to Your voice and align myself with Your will in every area of my life. God, replace my doubts with hope, my fears with faith, and my pride with humility. I acknowledge that I've been trying to figure things out on my own, but I now realize that trusting and obeying Your word is the key to my breakthrough and salvation. Lord, come into my life and stir things up, even if it means stepping out of my comfort zone to make the changes You have in store for me. In Jesus' name, I pray. Amen!

I Surrender

Lord, I come to You head bowed down, broken, defeated, carrying the burdens of the world and seeking Your guidance, peace, protection, comfort, and strength. In my time of need, I ask that You grant me the wisdom of Solomon, the boldness and the heart of David, the patience of Job, the strength of Samson, the humility of John the Baptist, and the faith of Abraham. For I know trouble doesn't last always, and I must walk by faith and not by sight. In my darkest hours, I pray that you grant me the ability to accept the things I can not change, the courage to change the things I can change, and the wisdom to know the difference, for you are God and God alone! In Jesus' name, I pray. Amen!

Break Every Chain

Heavenly Father, as I embark upon my spiritual journey, I am surrounded by moments of doubt, fear, worry, and weakness that the enemy attempts to bestow upon me. It is written in Ephesians 6:12: 'For our struggle is not against flesh and blood, but against the powers of this dark world and against the spiritual forces of evil in the heavenly realms.' Lord, I come to You humble as I know how, asking You to release the shackles from my feet and the burdens of my heart. I ask You to break generational curses, restore hope, and comfort me with Your Holy Spirit. Shape me, mold me, strengthen me, and carry me through the trials and tribulations of life. Renew my spirit. I declare victory over the enemy and the weight of the world. In Jesus' name, I pray. Amen!

A Mother's Prayer

Lord, my heart is heavy, my eyes are overflowing with tears, and I am acting as an intercessor for my child. For I know that you have given each of us the choice to make our own decisions, but I ask your forgiveness for his selfish decisions and wrongdoings that are a result of earthly desires and temptations. For it is written in Proverbs 22:26 - Train up a child in the way he should go; even when he is old, he will not depart from it. I pray that Satan's false promises and deceit do not lead him to condemnation and eternal suffering, for you are the good shepherd who left 99 sheep to find the lost one. The fourth man in the fire, for you are always in the room. Protect him, cover him, free him from the bondage that has been self-afflicted, and cleanse his soul. In Jesus' name, I pray. Amen

Purpose

Heavenly Father, I submit myself to you. I know that each of us has a purpose in life as it pertains to the upbuilding of your kingdom. Lord, I know I have a calling on my life; however, I am not sure how You wish to use me. I ask that You reveal to me my calling and order my footsteps. I pray that you help me to get out of my own way and allow me to see clearly what You would have me see. You will be the land between my feet and the light in my path. In Jesus' name, I pray. Amen!

Contact me by email! Let's pray together.

Thank you for your support!

t@prophetesstasha.com